I0476865

GLOBAL MARITIME PIRACY:
FUELING TERRORISM, HARMING TRADE

HEARING

BEFORE THE

SUBCOMMITTEE ON TERRORISM, NONPROLIFERATION, AND TRADE

OF THE

COMMITTEE ON FOREIGN AFFAIRS
HOUSE OF REPRESENTATIVES

ONE HUNDRED TWELFTH CONGRESS

FIRST SESSION

JUNE 15, 2011

Serial No. 112–41

Printed for the use of the Committee on Foreign Affairs

U.S. GOVERNMENT PRINTING OFFICE

66–901PDF WASHINGTON : 2011

For sale by the Superintendent of Documents, U.S. Government Printing Office
Internet: bookstore.gpo.gov Phone: toll free (866) 512–1800; DC area (202) 512–1800
Fax: (202) 512–2104 Mail: Stop IDCC, Washington, DC 20402–0001

COMMITTEE ON FOREIGN AFFAIRS

ILEANA ROS-LEHTINEN, Florida, *Chairman*

CHRISTOPHER H. SMITH, New Jersey
DAN BURTON, Indiana
ELTON GALLEGLY, California
DANA ROHRABACHER, California
DONALD A. MANZULLO, Illinois
EDWARD R. ROYCE, California
STEVE CHABOT, Ohio
RON PAUL, Texas
MIKE PENCE, Indiana
JOE WILSON, South Carolina
CONNIE MACK, Florida
JEFF FORTENBERRY, Nebraska
MICHAEL T. McCAUL, Texas
TED POE, Texas
GUS M. BILIRAKIS, Florida
JEAN SCHMIDT, Ohio
BILL JOHNSON, Ohio
DAVID RIVERA, Florida
MIKE KELLY, Pennsylvania
TIM GRIFFIN, Arkansas
TOM MARINO, Pennsylvania
JEFF DUNCAN, South Carolina
ANN MARIE BUERKLE, New York
RENEE ELLMERS, North Carolina
VACANT

HOWARD L. BERMAN, California
GARY L. ACKERMAN, New York
ENI F.H. FALEOMAVAEGA, American
    Samoa
DONALD M. PAYNE, New Jersey
BRAD SHERMAN, California
ELIOT L. ENGEL, New York
GREGORY W. MEEKS, New York
RUSS CARNAHAN, Missouri
ALBIO SIRES, New Jersey
GERALD E. CONNOLLY, Virginia
THEODORE E. DEUTCH, Florida
DENNIS CARDOZA, California
BEN CHANDLER, Kentucky
BRIAN HIGGINS, New York
ALLYSON SCHWARTZ, Pennsylvania
CHRISTOPHER S. MURPHY, Connecticut
FREDERICA WILSON, Florida
KAREN BASS, California
WILLIAM KEATING, Massachusetts
DAVID CICILLINE, Rhode Island

YLEEM D.S. POBLETE, *Staff Director*
RICHARD J. KESSLER, *Democratic Staff Director*

———

SUBCOMMITTEE ON TERRORISM, NONPROLIFERATION, AND TRADE

EDWARD R. ROYCE, California, *Chairman*

TED POE, Texas
JEFF DUNCAN, South Carolina
BILL JOHNSON, Ohio
TIM GRIFFIN, Arkansas
ANN MARIE BUERKLE, New York
RENEE ELLMERS, North Carolina

BRAD SHERMAN, California
DAVID CICILLINE, Rhode Island
GERALD E. CONNOLLY, Virginia
BRIAN HIGGINS, New York
ALLYSON SCHWARTZ, Pennsylvania

CONTENTS

GLOBAL MARITIME PIRACY: FUELING TERRORISM, HARMING TRADE

WEDNESDAY, JUNE 15, 2011

House of Representatives,
Subcommittee on Terrorism,
Nonproliferation, and Trade,
Committee on Foreign Affairs,
Washington, DC.

The subcommittee met, pursuant to notice, at 2:05 p.m., in room 2172, Rayburn House Office Building, Hon. Edward R. Royce (chairman of the subcommittee) presiding.

Mr. ROYCE. This subcommittee hearing will come to order. Today's subcommittee hearing is entitled "Global Maritime Piracy: Fueling Terrorism, Harming Trade."

And this hearing of the Subcommittee on Terrorism, Non-proliferation, and Trade is going to look at a problem that is not a new problem on this planet. The Romans branded pirates outlaws of humanity, and they punished them severely, as did the British and certainly us. In our country's early history, we forcefully, we very decisively confronted pirate attacks off the Barbary Coast.

But today, we face a very different situation. Today, maritime piracy is booming without any credible deterrence, without the type of deterrence you saw at one point in time from the British Navy or from the U.S. fleet. As we speak, there are 27 vessels and 449 hostages being held by Somali pirates. We have some slides up on the monitor there, if you would like to take a look, that tell a tale.

From 2007 to 2010, hijackings and pirate attacks increased sevenfold. Employing mother ships, pirates now operate in a space of 2.5 million square nautical miles, over double the territory from just 2 years ago.

In January, a U.N. official declared, "Pirates are becoming the masters of the Indian Ocean." And the number and abuse of hostages has increased dramatically.

More attacks and more hostages, of course, equal greater ransom payments. The average ransom payment was $300,000 a few years ago. Today the average is $4 million to $5 million. For Somali pirates, crime does pay.

We should be concerned that these payments may fund al-Shabaab, al-Qaeda's East Africa arm. We cannot be passive. As Leon Panetta testified last week, al-Shabaab's threat "to the U.S. homeland is significant and on the rise."

The United States has begun targeting pirate ring leaders. In April, FBI agents entered Somalia. We apprehended an individual

(1)

who oversaw ransom negotiations for four American hostages who were killed. This was a first. One pirate leader is out the game. That is good.

Unfortunately, there are many, many more to go.

Pirate "investors," as they call themselves, investors, who back attacks, span the globe. There are pirate investors in Europe, in the Middle East, and in Australia. Piracy has become a vast criminal enterprise. We must track down these criminals. The GAO has given the administration poor marks on tracking pirate financing. That has to change.

Many navies are working to deter piracy in the Gulf of Aden, but as Secretary Clinton recently remarked, we are not getting enough out of it.

Too many of our partners are there to log sea time instead of stopping pirates. That is my quote, not hers, that second part of that, just for the record.

The pendulum between the Romans and our 21st century treatment of pirates, frankly, has swung too far in the direction of favoring the pirates. Extreme notions of human rights and the rights of the accused mean today that of the 10 pirates we catch, 9 are then released.

I prefer the justice our SEALs dispensed against three pirates 2 years ago. That is a credible deterrence. When navies are used to forcefully take out piracy, that is a credible deterrence.

The U.N. is pushing for specialized piracy courts. The Obama administration, once opposed, is now actively considering this proposal. I have a hard time justifying an international justice system for pirates. But we will hear the administration's case.

Lastly, it should be stressed that industry itself can do much to prevent piracy. Shippers are often blasé about ransom payments, and it is the vessels that do not employ best management practices that are the ones that are hijacked.

And I want everybody to think about this: Not a single ship employing armed guards has been successfully pirated. Not one. As we will hear, we are throwing a lot at this problem, even putting American lives at risk. Industry has to play its part in this.

I will now turn to the ranking member for a 5-minute opening statement, and then we will go to other members and then our witnesses.

[The prepared statement of Mr. Royce follows:]

Subcommittee on Terrorism, Nonproliferation, and Trade
Global Maritime Piracy: Fueling Terrorism, Harming Trade
Chairman Ed Royce
June 15, 2011

Piracy is not a new problem. The Romans branded pirates outlaws of humanity and punished them severely. In our country's early history, we forcefully, and decisively, confronted pirate attacks off the Barbary Coast.

Today, maritime piracy is booming. As we speak, 23 vessels and 439 hostages are being held by Somali pirates.

As the slides on the monitor show, from 2007 to 2010, hijackings increased sevenfold.

Employing "mother ships," pirates now operate in a space of 2.5 million square nautical miles, over double the territory from two years ago. In January, a U.N. official declared: "pirates are becoming the masters of the Indian Ocean." The number and abuse of hostages has increased.

More attacks and more hostages equals greater ransom payments. The average ransom payment of $300,000 a few years ago has become $4-5 million today. For Somali pirates, crime does pay...

We should be concerned that these payments may fund al-Shabaab, al-Qaeda's East Africa arm. We can't be passive. As Leon Panetta testified last week, al-Sahbaab's threat "to the U.S. homeland is significant and on the rise."

The United States has begun targeting pirate ringleaders. In April, FBI agents entered Somalia and apprehended an individual who oversaw ransom negotiations for four American hostages who were killed. This was a first. One pirate leader is out of the game. Good.

Unfortunately, there are many more to go. Pirate "investors" who back attacks span the globe – Europe, the Middle East or Australia. Piracy has become a vast criminal enterprise. We must track down these criminals. The GAO has given the Administration poor marks on tracking pirate financing. That has to change.

Many navies are working to deter piracy in the Gulf of Aden. But as Secretary Clinton recently remarked, we are not getting enough out of it. Too many of our partners are there to log sea time, instead of stopping pirates.

The pendulum between the Romans and our 21st century treatment of pirates has swung too far in favor of the pirates. Extreme notions of human rights and the rights of the accused mean that 9 out of 10 pirates are caught – and then released. I prefer the justice our SEALs dispensed against three pirates two years ago.

The lack of prosecution has led to a U.N. push for specialized piracy courts. The Obama Administration, once opposed, is now actively considering this proposal. I have a hard time justifying an international justice system for pirates. But we'll hear the Administration's case.

Lastly, it should be stressed that industry itself can do much to prevent piracy. Shippers are often blasé about ransom payments. And it is the vessels that do not employ best management practices that are hijacked. Not a single ship employing armed guards has been successfully pirated. As we'll hear, we are throwing a lot at this problem – even putting American lives at risk. Industry has to play its part.

Mr. SHERMAN. Thank you, Mr. Chairman, for convening these hearings.

I know we are going the hear excellent testimony from the representative of the Department of Defense. I know that not only from his reputation but from his Aunt Winnie.

I want to thank you for calling these hearings, thank our witness for being here. I have been an advocate of burden sharing for quite some time. I think that we undercut our burden sharing efforts by deliberately understating the cost of our international operations, whether they be aid or especially military operations.

In an effort to understate the cost to the American people, we understate the cost to the world. We use the marginal cost system of accounting for determining the cost of these operations, and any perusing of a cost accounting book would say that that is the worst possible system to use for calculating cost. Full cost accounting ought to be used, and on that basis, we are doing far more to aid those actions urged on us by the U.N. than we currently claim credit for.

It is not cheap to maintain a military capable of responding to piracies, tsunamis and other disasters around the world.

I think Secretary Gates' comments that our European allies have not only hollowed out their militaries but are now contemplating even greater cuts comes to mind.

When we look at global piracy, we do see some 60 nations involved, including some that are not our traditional allies. But there are discouraging signs, as the chairman points out. Some 90 percent of the pirates are part of the catch-and-release program. This is absurd. We ought to be willing to extradite these pirates to whichever nation in the world will treat them with the most justice. And there is universal jurisdiction. If our European friends are unwilling to impose penalties, that does not mean they have to release the pirates.

Piracy, of course, as I mentioned, has universal jurisdiction.

We also ought to look at how the shipowners are behaving. Should we be requiring armed guards? Should we be prohibiting ransom? Or should we let them view ransom and detention as just a cost of business?

This understates the cost of piracy. The cost of piracy is not just the ransom. It is not just the delay. This money is going to some of the worst people in the world who are either killing more people on the high seas or killing more people in Somalia.

Paying ransom and refusing to invest in safety is not a business decision. And it is not a decision we should allow businesses to make on a strictly profit-and-loss basis.

I have so much more to say, but in so many other occasions, my opening statements have stretched the limit of the definition of 5 minutes, and I am going to yield back for this one time this year. Thank you.

Mr. ROYCE. Well, I thank the ranking member for yielding.

I will make two other brief points just for the edification of the committee members. The Kenyan Government estimates that 30 percent of ransom payments are funneled to al-Shabaab. And Shabaab commanders have spoken of a sea Jihad and have opened a marine office, a marine office to coordinate with pirates.

We will go now to Judge Poe of Texas for 2 minutes.

Mr. POE. Thank you, Mr. Chairman.

The pirates are back. These aren't swashbuckling, eye-patch wearing pirates. These are modern-day pirates that have automatic weapons, elaborate intelligence systems, sophisticated money laundering network in connections to their brothers in crime, Islamic terrorists.

One of my constituents from Texas, Bill Rouse, is an avid sailor of the high seas, but he is just one example of the way these pirate thugs have taken away his freedom. He, like many other small boat owners that cross the ocean, have to get a barge to put their ship on or their boat on to go through pirate-filled areas.

The pirates are in it for the money. About 40 percent of the world's oil is shipped through the Indian Ocean, where the Somali pirates have had a field day. Collectively governments spend $1 billion a year policing the pirates while the cost of piracy to the global economy is anywhere from $7 billion to $12 billion.

The industry is growing. New reports from confirmed Somali pirates reach all the way to the west coast of India, spanning the breadth of the Indian Ocean. I have here a poster of some of the recent—excuse me, Mr. Duncan—the pirate attacks in the Indian Ocean. From Somalia to India is 2,240 miles. That is a long way. And all of these show pirate attacks. The red are 19 months prior to October, but the blue, the most of them, are just from October to February of this year. They are increasing, and they are, with reckless abandon, moving closer and closer to India.

Right now, I understand there are approximately 200 small boat owners in Malaysia waiting to go west but can't get there because they are afraid of the pirates. There are a couple hundred more in the Pacific Ocean waiting to go west, but they cannot, because they are afraid of the pirates.

Last year Somalian pirates hijacked 53 ships and a total of 1,100 hostages were held for ransom. This is increasing every day, and they act with disregard to anyone, especially to nations that should be patrolling the high seas.

We can take control of this situation if we have the moral will to do so. We can lower the benefits by pirates by stopping them from receiving money. We can raise the cost just like Jefferson did to the pirates off the shores of Tripoli in 1801. The Constitution actually gives authority to the United States Government to do something about piracy, Article I, Section 8, to define and punish pirates, piracy, and felonies committed on the high seas. It is time the United States takes some action and put these outlaws on the high seas out of business and send them to Davy Jones' locker. I yield back.

Mr. ROYCE. Thank you, Mr. Poe.

We will go to Mr. Higgins of New York for 3 minutes.

Mr. HIGGINS. Thank you, Mr. Chairman.

Obviously, this is a big problem in that piracy has grown to a multi-million dollar criminal enterprise and pirates attack or seize ships. Ransoms now average between $4 million and $5 million. And some 2,000 pirates operate from Somalia's shores.

Larger pirate syndicates are becoming increasingly more sophisticated and professional. They seize cargo ships and oil tankers because of their huge ransom values.

Piracy thrives in Somalia for two reasons: Somalia is one of the world's most failed states; and Somalia is a desperately poor state, and there is huge money in pirating.

My concern also is where this money ends up. And so I look forward to the testimony of our expert witnesses and drilling deeper into this problem and hopefully coming up with some answers.

With that, I yield back.

Mr. ROYCE. Mr. Duncan.

Mr. DUNCAN. Thank you, Mr. Chairman. I will be brief.

This is a real issue. I just came back where I talked with the Pacific Command. A conversation we had was about piracy, growing threat of piracy around the world. We had the opportunity to talk with some folks in the Philippines about the issue and about the Malacca Strait and how the pirates are starting to come further and further east, as Judge Poe said, off the coast of India and even closer to Indonesia. So I certainly appreciate the hearing today.

I came to learn. I am a freshman Member of Congress. That is part of the reason I went and talked with those folks about these issues. And I look forward to hearing your testimony today. And I yield back.

Mr. ROYCE. Very good. We are joined by representatives of the State and Defense Departments today.

Andrew Shapiro is the Assistant Secretary of State for Political-Military Affairs. He served on the Obama transition team and, prior to that, was Senator Clinton's senior defense and foreign policy adviser. Mr. Shapiro received a joint law and master's in international affairs degree from Columbia University.

William Wechsler is the Deputy Assistant Secretary of Defense for Counternarcotics and Global Threats, where he leads the department's counternarcotics and threat finance policies and operations around the world. He reports to the Assistant Secretary of Defense for Special Operations, Low-Intensity Conflict. Previously, Mr. Wechsler served as special adviser to the Secretary of the Treasury on the staff of the National Security Council as director for transnational threats.

All of the witnesses' complete written testimony we have and have read, and will be entered in the record. I will remind our witnesses to summarize your statements, keep it to 5 minutes, if you can, and then we will go to questions.

And we will begin with Assistant Secretary Shapiro.

STATEMENT OF THE HONORABLE ANDREW J. SHAPIRO, ASSISTANT SECRETARY, BUREAU OF POLITICAL-MILITARY AFFAIRS, U.S. DEPARTMENT OF STATE

Mr. SHAPIRO. Chairman Royce, Ranking Member Sherman members of the committee, I appreciate this opportunity to testify about the problem of piracy on the high seas and outline our new approach to combat this scourge.

As all the members of the committee noted during their opening statements, piracy off the coast of Somalia is a crime of growing concern. The number of pirate attacks has risen steadily since

2007. In 2010, Somali pirates captured over 1,000 sailors aboard 49 vessels. As of June 14th of this year, 400 seafarers were being held as hostages and 18 hijacked ships were being held for ransom.

The increase in the total number of attacks has tragically come with an increase in the level of violence against hostages. This was displayed in brutal fashion by the killing of the four American citizens aboard the sailing vessel Quest in February.

Pirates are also evolving their tactics. Through the use of mother ships and GPS technology, pirates have been able to expand their geographic range from the southern Red Sea to the eastern Indian ocean. Mother ships are hijacked ships used as floating bases, which allow pirates to stage attacks hundreds of miles from Somali coast.

A vicious cycle has formed where ever rising ransom payments have not just spurred additional pirate activity but have also enabled pirates to increase their operational capabilities and sophistication.

Piracy has gone from a fairly ad hoc, disorganized criminal endeavor to a highly developed, transnational criminal enterprise.

In response, the United States has taken the lead in pursuing a multilateral and multidimensional approach to combating piracy emanating from the Coast of Somalia. Piracy can only be effectively addressed through broad, coordinated and comprehensive international efforts.

In January 2009, the United States helped establish the Contact Group on Piracy off the Coast of Somalia which now includes nearly 70 nations, international organizations and maritime trade associations.

The Contact Group helps coordinate national and international counterpiracy policies and actions. It has galvanized action and harmonized counterpiracy policy among participating countries and international organizations. There is immense international concern over piracy and an increasing willingness amongst affected nations to expand counterpiracy efforts and increase cooperation and collaboration with the United States.

With this multilateral framework in place, we have pursued a multidimensional approach that focuses on security, prevention, and deterrence.

Improving security on the seas has been a principal focus of our efforts. As pirate tactics have grown more sophisticated and aggressive, the international naval forces performing counterpiracy operations have responded in kind. U.S. Naval Forces have thwarted pirate attacks in process, engaged pirate skiffs and mother ships and successfully taken back hijacked ships by opposed boardings.

U.S. Naval Forces Central Command (NAVCENT) has worked with partners to set up a 463-mile long corridor through the Gulf of Aden called the Internationally Recommended Transit Corridor or IRTC for short.

This transit zone has been successful in reducing the number of attacks within the corridor, but it has had the unfortunate side effect of pushing pirate activities elsewhere outside of the corridor. Given the immense area in which pirates operate, it is often impossible for naval forces to respond in time to stop an attack. There is just too much water to patrol.

That is why the United States has also focused on prevention by encouraging commercial and private vessels to implement industry developed best management practices. These are practical steps shipowners and seafarers can take to prevent pirate attacks from happening in the first place.

More flagged states are also allowing armed guards on merchant vessels. It is notable, as the chairman mentioned, that no vessel with an armed security team embarked has been successfully hijacked.

It is also U.S. policy to discourage the payment of ransoms and to seek to deny pirates the benefits of any ransoms which may be paid.

Lastly, to deter piracy, we have sought to expand prosecution and incarceration. When suspected pirates have been captured, the United States has consistently advocated that the states directly victimized take on the responsibility to not only try these suspects but to also incarcerate them if convicted. There are more than 1,000 pirates in custody in more than 18 countries where national prosecutions are taking place.

Taken in concert, this multilateral or multi dimensional approach seems to have led to a drop in successful pirate attacks. But total number of successful attacks in March, April and May of this year was eight. This is still unacceptably high, but it is down significantly from the 27 successful attacks for the same 3-month period in 2010.

This is a small sample size, so we do not know for sure if it signifies a turning of the tide or a brief aberration. But even if these figures do point to significant progress, given the lucrative financial incentives, pirates will likely attempt to further adapt their approaches.

Since pirates are already adapting and expanding their efforts, we must as well.

Earlier this year, Secretary Clinton expressed impatience with the lack of progress against piracy and urged that more be done to address this scourge.

After an intensive review of our strategy following the Quest tragedy, Secretary Clinton approved a series of recommendations which, taken together, constitute a new strategic approach. This approach calls for continuing naval action at sea as well as exploring nonmilitary options to target pirate leaders and organizers ashore.

Our intention is to pursue innovative measures to maximize all the tools at our disposal in order to disrupt the activities of the financiers, organizer and logistics suppliers of piracy. We are in the process of discussing our ideas for these new lines of action with our interagency partners with an eye toward rapid implementation of agreed measures.

The focus on network is essential. As piracy has evolved into an organized transnational criminal enterprise, it is increasingly clear that the arrest and prosecution of pirates captured at sea, who are often the low-level operatives involved in piracy, is insufficient on its own to meet our longer-term counterpiracy goals. Pirate leaders and facilitators receive income both from investors and ransom payments and disburse a portion of the proceeds of ransom back to their investors and to the pirates who actually hijack the ships and hold the crews hostage.

We will focus in the coming months in identifying, apprehending the criminal conspirators who provide the leadership and financial management of the pirate enterprise with the objective of bringing them to trial and interrupting pirate business processes.

Already the United States has recently indicted and extradited two alleged Somali pirate negotiators for the respective leadership roles in attacks on U.S. vessels.

To achieve this, we are working to connect law enforcement communities, intelligence agencies, financial experts and our international partners to promote information sharing and develop actionable information against pirate conspirators. This effort includes tracking pirate sources of financing and supplies, such as fuel, outboard motors and weapons.

Additionally an important element of our recalibrated counterpiracy approach involves renewed emphasis on enhancing the capacity of the international community and particularly states in the region to prosecute and incarcerate suspected pirates.

The United States supports a comprehensive approach that addresses concerns about incarceration and repatriation by increasing prison capacity in Somalia, developing a framework for prisoner transfers so convicted pirates serve their sentence back in their home country of Somalia, and by working to establish a specialized piracy chamber in the national courts of one or more regional states.

Finally, we believe supporting the reestablishment of stability and adequate governance in Somalia represents the only sustainable long-term solution to piracy. This will require concentrated and coordinated assistance to states in the region, including those parts of Somali society with which we can work, to build their capacity to deal with the social, legal, economic and operational challenges to effective law enforcement.

However, acknowledging the difficult situation ashore does not preclude progress at sea. Through the State Department's new strategic approach, significant progress can be made to degrade the ability of pirates to conduct attacks and threaten vital shipping lanes.

We should have no illusions. There is no simple solution to modern day piracy off the Horn of Africa. But through the shared commitment of the United States and the international community, there is much we can do in the months and years ahead to achieve progress against this growing challenge. Thank you.

[The prepared statement of Mr. Shapiro follows:]

UNCLASSIFIED

Testimony
Assistant Secretary Andrew Shapiro
Bureau of Political-Military Affairs
U.S. Department of State
Before the House Committee on Foreign Affairs'
Sub-Committee on Terrorism, Nonproliferation and Trade
Hearing on "Confronting Global Piracy"
June 15, 2011, 2:00PM

Chairman Royce, Ranking Member Sherman, Members of the Committee: I
appreciate this opportunity to testify about the problem of piracy on the high seas
and outline our approach to combat this scourge.

As you are aware, piracy off the coast of Somalia is a crime of growing global
concern. Heavily-armed pirates board unarmed vessels and seize the ship, cargo
and crew for ransom. The lives of innocent seafarers have been lost and crew
members may be held hostage for many months, sometimes more than a year, in
appalling conditions. The monetary total of ransoms demanded runs into hundreds
of millions of dollars a year, with the total cost of piracy to the global economy
estimated to be in the billions.

A vicious cycle has formed where ever-rising ransom payments have not just
spurred additional pirate activity, but have also enabled pirates to increase their
operational capabilities and sophistication. Piracy has gone from a fairly ad hoc
disorganized criminal endeavor to a highly developed transnational criminal
enterprise.

The number of pirate attacks has risen steadily since 2007. In 2010, Somali pirates
captured over 1,000 sailors aboard 49 vessels. As of June 14, 400 seafarers were
being held as hostages, and 18 hijacked ships were being held for ransom. Pirate
attacks were highest in January and February of this year. The increase in the total
number of attacks has been tragically accompanied by an increase in the level of
violence against hostages, as displayed in brutal fashion by the killing of the four
American Citizens aboard the sailing vessel QUEST in February.

Piracy has become more organized, more violent and has expanded to cover an
increasingly large geographic area, from the southern Red Sea to the eastern Indian
Ocean. Evolving tactics, such as the use of "motherships" -- hijacked ships used as
floating bases from which to stage attacks hundreds of miles from the Somali coast
-- and technology such as GPS, have extended the pirates' geographic range.

- 2 -

Somali pirates now operate in a total sea space of approximately 2.5 million square nautical miles, an increase from approximately 1 million square nautical miles two years ago.

In response, the United States has taken the lead in pursuing a multilateral and multidimensional approach to combating piracy emanating from the coast of Somalia.

Piracy affects the international community as a whole and can only be effectively addressed through broad, coordinated, and comprehensive international efforts. The United States has, from the beginning, adopted a multilateral approach. In January 2009, we helped establish the Contact Group on Piracy off the Coast of Somalia (Contact Group), which now includes nearly 70 nations, international organizations, and maritime trade associations, to help coordinate national and international counter-piracy policies and actions. The Contact Group has proven effective in galvanizing action and harmonizing counter-piracy policy among participating countries and organizations, including the United Nations, NATO, and the European Union. There is immense international concern over piracy and an increasing willingness amongst affected nations to expand counter-piracy efforts and increase cooperation and collaboration with the United States.

With this multilateral framework in place, we have pursued a multi-dimensional approach that focuses on security – through the projection of military power to defend commercial and private vessels; prevention – through encouraging the private sector to adopt self-protection measures; and deterrence – through effective prosecution and incarceration.

Improving security on the seas has been a principal focus of our efforts. As pirate tactics have grown more sophisticated and aggressive, the international naval forces performing counter-piracy operations have responded in kind. U.S. naval forces have thwarted pirate attacks in-process, engaged pirate skiffs and "motherships," and successfully taken back hijacked ships by opposed boardings.

The United States established Combined Task Force 151 -- a multinational task force charged with conducting counter-piracy naval patrols in the Gulf of Aden and off the eastern coast of Somalia, covering an area of more than one million square miles. In addition to this effort, there are a number of other coordinated multi-national naval patrols off the Horn of Africa. NATO is engaging in Operation Ocean Shield, the European Union has Operation ATALANTA, and other national navies in the area conduct counter-piracy patrols as well. On any

- 3 -

given day up to 30 vessels from as many as 20 nations are engaged in counter-piracy operations in the region, including countries new to these kinds of efforts such as China, India and Japan.

U.S. Naval Forces Central Command (NAVCENT) has also worked with partners to set up a 463 mile-long corridor through the Gulf of Aden, called the Internationally Recommended Transit Corridor or IRTC for short. This transit zone for commercial shipping is heavily patrolled by naval forces and has been successful in reducing the number of attacks within the corridor. But it also has had the unfortunate side effect of pushing pirate activities elsewhere, outside of the corridor.

Naval operations are necessary but not sufficient for a comprehensive counter-piracy strategy. Given the immense area in which pirates operate, it is often impossible for naval forces to respond in time to stop an attack. There is just too much water to patrol.

That is why the United States has also focused on prevention, by encouraging commercial and private vessels to implement industry-developed "best management practices" – practical steps shipowners and seafarers can take to prevent pirate attacks from happening in the first place. These measures include steps like: proceeding at full speed through high risk areas; placing additional lookouts on watches; and employing physical barriers such as razor wire. More flag states are also allowing armed guards on merchant vessels. It is notable that no vessel with an armed security team embarked has been successfully hijacked.

It is also U.S. policy to discourage the payment of ransoms, and to seek to deny pirates the benefits of any ransoms which may be paid. Nevertheless, shipowners and operators, as well as concerned families, have continued to pay ransoms to free crewmembers and release ships. As more and larger ransoms have been paid, pirate demands have increased and the average ransom amount has roughly doubled in the last three years. We encourage flag states, shipowners and private parties involved in hostage crises to seek assistance from appropriate U.S. government sources in their crisis management procedures.

Lastly, to deter piracy, we have sought to expand prosecution and incarceration. When suspected pirates have been captured, and there has been sufficient evidence to support pursuing a prosecution, the United States has consistently advocated that they be tried, and incarcerated if convicted, by the states directly victimized by the attack, including the flag state or the state of nationality of the owner or crew. The

- 4 -

United States has successfully prosecuted accused pirates in its federal courts and more pirates are currently on trial. Other coalition forces have followed America's lead in taking action when feasible to free pirated ships and rescue hostage crews, and transferred suspected pirates back to their capitals for prosecution.

Taken in concert, this multilateral and multi-dimensional approach seems to have led to a drop in successful of pirate attacks. The total number of successful attacks in March, April and May of this year was eight. This is still unacceptably high but is down significantly from the 27 successful attacks for the same three-month period in 2010. This is a small sample size so we do not know for sure if this signifies a turning of the tide or a brief aberration. But even if these figures do point to significant progress, given the significant financial incentives for piracy, pirates will likely attempt to further adapt their approaches.

We are seeing this already. Pirates are now adapting their tactics in response to the increased tempo and effectiveness of international naval operations. For example, pirates holding a merchant vessel agreed to release the ship's Indian crew after receiving a $3.5 million ransom recently. Instead, the pirates released only eight of the 15 hostages and demanded India free 120 suspected pirates captured by the Indian navy earlier this year, vowing to hold onto any Indian nationals taken until then.

Since pirates are already adapting and expanding their efforts, we must as well. Expanded action is no doubt needed. Earlier this year, Secretary Clinton expressed impatience with the lack of progress against piracy and affirmed that more needed to be done to address this scourge. Following the Quest tragedy in February, Secretary Clinton directed an intensive review of our counter-piracy posture and approved a series of recommendations which we are seeking to implement.

The State Department's approach calls for continuing naval actions at sea, as well as exploring non-military options to target pirate leaders and organizers ashore. Our intention is to pursue innovative measures to maximize our diplomatic, judicial, economic, and developmental tools in order to disrupt the activities of the financiers, organizers and logistics suppliers of piracy. We are in the process of discussing our ideas for these new lines of action with our Interagency partners, with an eye to rapid implementation of agreed measures.

The focus ashore is essential, as piracy has evolved into an organized transnational criminal enterprise conducted for profit. It is increasingly clear that the arrest and prosecution of pirates captured at sea – often the low-level operatives involved in piracy – is insufficient, on its own, to meet our longer term counter-piracy goals. To maintain the momentum and space for action gained by naval operations, we have begun an effort to identify ways to disrupt these criminal networks and to determine the means to dismantle their supporting financial networks.

We intend to work with our international partners in the coming months to go after the smaller number of criminal conspirators who provide the leadership and financial management of the pirate enterprise, with the objective of bringing them to trial. The United States recently indicted and apprehended two alleged Somali pirate negotiators for their respective leadership roles in the attack on the QUEST and on a Danish vessel carrying U.S.-owned cargo.

Tracking financial flows provides an expanded understanding of the networks of leaders, organizers and financiers behind piracy and is critical to interrupting pirate business processes. With the application of mapping techniques developed in recent years, we believe that we can gradually build a good understanding of the networks that organize, finance, and profit from piracy. Pirate leaders and facilitators receive income both from investors and ransom payments, and disburse a portion of the proceeds of ransoms back to their investors and to the pirates who actually hijack the ships and hold the crews hostage.

We are working with are international partners to connect law enforcement communities, intelligence agencies, financial experts to promote information sharing and develop actionable information against pirate conspirators for prosecution and to stimulate additional intelligence collection on their networks. This effort includes identifying pirate leaders, tracking their sources of financing and supplies such as fuel, outboard motors and weapons, disrupting those support networks, and ensuring these leaders and facilitators of piracy are known to law enforcement officials in every country in which they do business.

This effort demands effective international cooperation. We are working with the international community to ensure that law enforcement and intelligence agencies tasked with counter-piracy responsibilities can collect, analyze, and share operational and financial information. Law enforcement officials must be able to share information gathered in the course of criminal investigations with intelligence officials to stimulate additional collection. Targeting financing may also involve adopting national legislation where necessary to criminalize the ways that conspirators are involved in piracy, including by using anti-conspiracy laws and laws that criminalize the financing of crime. It also demands prosecuting pirate

- 6 -

organizers, financiers, and facilitators, as well as lower-level pirates, in national courts.

Disrupting piracy financial flows has been a topic of discussion in the Contact Group since its creation. On March 1, 2011, the United States hosted the first Ad Hoc Meeting on the financial aspects of piracy off the coast of Somalia to discuss mechanisms by which the international community could undertake to address this aspect of Somali piracy. The Government of Italy has agreed to chair an informal working group to develop actionable projects to disrupt pirate financial flows, and a small group of like-minded countries ("Core Group") met in Rome just last week on June 8 to develop initiatives to be taken on the issue. The Republic of South Korea will convene a second Ad Hoc Meeting in Seoul on June 29 to expand on and formalize the work begun in the Core Group, and to lay the groundwork for its adoption and approval at the 9th Plenary Meeting of the Contact Group on July 14. This international effort will complement existing channels and frameworks for international law enforcement cooperation, including mutual legal assistance and extradition treaties, to expand and improve international counter-piracy efforts.

Additionally, an important element of our recalibrated counter-piracy approach involves renewed emphasis on enhancing the capacity of the international community, and particularly states in the region, to prosecute and incarcerate suspected pirates. Too often pirates are simply released because of a lack of capacity to prosecute or incarcerate. The United States supports a comprehensive approach that addresses concerns about incarceration and repatriation by:

- increasing prison capacity in Somalia;
- developing frameworks for prisoner transfers to provide for the controlled transfer of convicted pirates back to Somalia to serve their sentences in their home county;
- and by working to establish a specialized piracy chamber in the national courts of one or more regional states.

The Republic of Seychelles, which is actively prosecuting pirates but has limited prison capacity, has concluded prisoner transfer arrangements with Somalia's Transitional Federal Government, as well as Puntland and Somaliland authorities. This framework provides a model that could potentially be replicated by other prosecuting states.

At the same time, we are continuing to encourage states to undertake their national responsibility to apprehend, prosecute and incarcerate pirates, as we have done.

- 7 -

The United States is currently prosecuting 28 individuals involved in attacks on U.S. vessels or cargo, including 15 defendants accused in connection with the attack on the S/V QUEST. Recently, ten of those 15 defendants pled guilty to piracy and other crimes and now face up to life in prison. These U.S. prosecutions are among the more than 1,000 pirates in custody in more than 18 countries where national prosecutions are taking place. Sadly, the supply of young men willing to attempt piracy is very large, and the capacity of the international community to absorb those captured into their judicial and penal systems must continue to expand.

Finally, combating piracy emanating from a failed state will require concentrated and coordinated assistance to states in the region – including those parts of Somali society with which we can work – to build their capacity to deal with the social, legal, economic and operational challenges to effective law enforcement. As part of our Dual Track approach to Somalia, we are expanding our engagement with regional authorities in Somalia, including Somaliland, Puntland, Galmudug, so as to achieve a greater direct impact on Somali society. Realistically, there will be no end to piracy at sea until there is some degree of political stability and economic recovery ashore in Somalia, including local governmental authorities with the ability to enforce law and order both on land and at sea. We believe supporting the re-establishment of stability and adequate governance in Somalia represents the only sustainable long-term solution to piracy.

However, acknowledging the difficult situation ashore does not preclude progress at sea. Through the State Department's new strategic approach, significant progress can be made to degrade the ability of pirates to conduct attacks and threaten vital shipping lanes. We should have no illusions: there is no simple solution to modern-day piracy off the Horn of Africa. But through the shared commitment of the United States and the international community there is much we can do in the months and years ahead to achieve progress against this growing challenge.

Mr. ROYCE. Thank you, Mr. Shapiro.
Mr. Wechsler.

STATEMENT OF MR. WILLIAM F. WECHSLER, DEPUTY ASSIST-ANT SECRETARY, COUNTERNARCOTICS AND GLOBAL THREATS, U.S. DEPARTMENT OF DEFENSE

Mr. WECHSLER. Thank you very much, Mr. Chairman, Representative Sherman and other distinguished members of the subcommittee. I will be brief. And one thing that I will skip in my oral statement is a description of the problem because, quite frankly, you all have described it extremely well and very accurately.

The cost of piracy is no more visible, though, than through the tragedy aboard the sailing vessel Quest in February. Four Americans—Jean and Scott Adam, Phyllis McKay, and Robert Riggle—were murdered by pirates.

Chairman Royce and Representative Sherman, I understand the Adams were from Marina del Rey in your State. This incident is a stark reminder of what is at stake in our efforts to fight the piracy.

One thing that has been mentioned is the question of the connections between the pirates and the revenues that they receive and terrorists that operate in the same area. This is an exceedingly important question.

I think it would be untrue if we were to represent to you that we know the answer to this question or that the intelligence on this issue is much less than any of us would like.

However, as we see it now, we believe that the terrorists and the pirates are not operationally or organizationally aligned, though there is an element of coercion that results in pirate revenues going to al-Shabaab.

Disrupting piracy will remain challenging for several reasons. First and foremost, as was just discussed by my colleague from the Department of State, the root causes of Somalia piracy lie in Somalia, in the poverty, instability and absence of governance in that country.

Second, Somali pirates operate in an area covering approximately 2.9 million square nautical miles. This is an area approximately the size of the continental United States. It is a vast amount of area that simply cannot be covered by naval forces. Indeed, if you took all of the navies of all of the countries in all of the world and put them against this area, we still wouldn't be able to cover this amount of nautical space.

Third, captured suspected pirates often go unprosecuted, as has been noted, even when significant criminal evidence exists. Many states lack the appropriate domestic laws to prosecute pirates. Other states may have the necessary legal frameworks but do not have the prosecutorial and judicial capacity to hold pirates accountable. And most troubling, other states just simply lack the political will at all to do this job.

Finally, as the members of this subcommittee know, the Department of Defense has many other urgent priorities around the world, particularly in Afghanistan and Iraq. In the Horn of Africa, many of the resources most in demand for counterpiracy activities, such as intelligence, surveillance and reconnaissance assets, are urgently required for counterterrorism purposes.

These multidimensional challenges illustrate that there is no simple solution to piracy. Most importantly, they underscore that this problem cannot be solved by military action alone.

Let me briefly describe the Department of Defense's role. Our primary role is to interrupt and terminate acts of piracy. We also play a supporting role in reducing the vulnerability of the maritime domain and facilitating the prosecution of suspected pirates.

On average, United States has two to four vessels participating in counterpiracy operations as part of Combined Task Force 151 and NATO's Operation Ocean Shield. Combined Task Force 151 is a component of combined maritime forces which regularly host international coordination meetings to share information and deconflict regional counterpiracy efforts.

The Department of Defense also is in support of the Departments of State and Treasury in efforts to track the finances and make this criminal activity less lucrative.

Mr. Chairman, I know that you have long and deep history in the efforts of the executive branch to combat threat finance and many other areas, and this is an area in which we all are committed to doing much more.

Through our interagency partners, DOD will continue to work with regional states to develop their capacity to patrol the seas and enhance their prosecutorial and judicial capabilities. While much remains to be done, as Assistant Secretary Shapiro has noted, we are seeing concrete results already from our efforts.

Since August 2008, international efforts have led to the destruction or confiscation of more than 100 pirate vessels and numerous weapons, including small arms and rocket-propelled grenades. The international community has also turned over approximately 1,000 pirates to various countries for prosecution.

From the Department of Defense's perspective, when we have the opportunity to act, we do act. But given the trends that you all described, it is, again, clear that military action is not enough.

As you noted, one of the—I will just close by noting that one of the very key elements in our strategy has to have a more effective shared responsibility with industry. Effectively countering piracy, the single most effective way to deter piracy in the short term is to make the vessels harder to attack successfully. There was a time a couple of years ago where there was some debate on this question. Best management practices, which range from hardening the vessel to maintaining professional civilian armed security teams on board, can thwart the majority of pirate attacks without the need for military intervention.

I would underscore, as you did, Mr. Chairman, that no vessel that has implemented best management practices and has armed private security teams aboard has been successfully pirated. Indeed, just last month, at least six attacks were halted after embarked security teams engaged pirates.

Thank you very much for inviting me to this hearing. I look forward to your questions, sir.

[The prepared statement of Mr. Wechsler follows:]

STATEMENT FOR THE RECORD

MR. WILLIAM F. WECHSLER

DEPUTY ASSISTANT SECRETARY OF DEFENSE

COUNTERNARCOTICS AND GLOBAL THREATS

U.S. DEPARTMENT OF DEFENSE

BEFORE THE

HOUSE COMMITTEE ON FOREIGN AFFAIRS

SUBCOMMITTEE ON

TERRORISM, NONPROLIFERATION, AND TRADE

JUNE 15, 2011

Mr. Chairman, Representative Sherman, and other distinguished members of the subcommittee, I appreciate this opportunity to testify about the problem of piracy in and around the Arabian Sea and western Indian Ocean.

Piracy is a growing threat, and we must acknowledge and confront the threats and challenges the piracy phenomenon poses. It is worth our efforts, however, to contextualize the problem: pirates attack less than one half of one percent of shipping in the Gulf of Aden, and those attacks are successful approximately one third of the time.

Unfortunately, it is also true that, over the last several years, we have seen an upswing in the number of reported pirate attacks worldwide and an expansion in the area of Somali pirate operations. As recently as 2007, the Gulf of Guinea off the coast of West Africa was the most active part of the world for piracy, but most pirate activity is now conducted by Somali pirates in the broader Horn of Africa region. These pirates operate from shore-based enclaves along the 1,880-mile Somali coastline, which is approximate to the distance from Portland, Maine to Miami, Florida. Since 2009, we have seen a decrease in the number of attacks carried out by Somali pirates in the Gulf of Aden. Unfortunately, their overall area of operations has increased. Somali pirates not only operate in the U.S. Central Command area of responsibility, but they now conduct attacks in both the U.S. Africa Command and U.S. Pacific Command areas of responsibility. Somali pirates operate in a total sea space of approximately 2.85 million square nautical miles – an area approximately the same size as the continental United States.

Somali pirates are less likely to operate in the Gulf of Aden as a result of the successful implementation of the Internationally Recommended Transit Corridor where U.S. and international forces regularly patrol. Instead, Somali pirates are using pirated ships – commonly deemed "motherships" – to expand their area of operations more than 1,500 nautical miles from the coast of Somalia as far east as the Kavaratti Islands near India, northward into the Gulf of Oman, and southward into the Mozambique Channel. As of June 7, Somali pirates hold 21 vessels and 481 crewmembers hostage.

Reducing incidents of piracy is important for both the United States and the international community. As a general matter, freedom of navigation is critical to our national security and international commerce, and it is also a core principle of customary international law as reflected in the Convention on the Law of the Sea and one that all nations have a stake in supporting. Piracy endangers innocent mariners and perpetuates instability ashore. Its hidden economic costs are also vast: in addition to ransom payments, the costs of ransom delivery, fees paid to negotiators, damage to ships, loss of ship hire, late delivery of cargo, and changes in the value of cargo can add millions of dollars to the overall cost of an act of piracy.

Recent incidents – including the heinous murder of the four Americans on the pirated sailing vessel (S/V) QUEST in February 2011 – continue to increase public and international attention to piracy. At the Department of Defense, we are working closely with other agencies and departments to develop and implement a comprehensive counter-piracy strategy.

The Department of Defense supports the National Security Council's "Countering Piracy off the Horn of Africa Partnership and Action Plan," in which our main role is to interrupt and terminate acts of piracy. We play a supporting role in preventing pirate attacks by reducing the vulnerability of the maritime domain, as well as ensuring that those who commit piratical acts are held accountable by facilitating the prosecution of suspected pirates by affected States, including in appropriate cases, by the United States.

The United States is not alone in this effort. More than 30 other nations have conducted or are currently conducting counter-piracy operations in the broader Horn of Africa region. Most countries participate in one of the three international coalitions: Combined Task Force 151 (CTF 151), NATO's Operation OCEAN SHIELD, and the European Union's Operation ATALANTA. The Combined Maritime Forces (CMF) regularly hosts Shared Awareness and Deconfliction (SHADE) meetings in Bahrain to provide a tactical and working-level opportunity for navies to come together to share information and deconflict counter-piracy efforts in the broader Horn of Africa region. The array of forces involved and their coordination efforts remain impressive. Several countries unaffiliated with these coalitions, such as China, India, and Japan, are also playing an increasingly important role in counter-piracy operations

On average, the United States has 1-2 vessels participating in counter-piracy operations as part of CTF 151. This multinational task force was established in January 2009 to conduct counter-piracy operations under a mission-based mandate throughout the CMF area of responsibility. In addition to the United States, the following 15 countries have participated in CTF 151: Australia, Bahrain, Canada, Denmark, France, Jordan, Netherlands, Pakistan, Republic of Korea, Saudi Arabia, Singapore, Spain, Thailand, Turkey, and the United Kingdom. CTF 151 is currently commanded by the Singapore Navy; in recent years, it has been commanded by the United States, Pakistan, Republic of Korea, and Turkey. The United States also participates in NATO's Operation OCEAN SHIELD.

We are seeing concrete results from our efforts. Since August 2008, international efforts have led to the destruction or confiscation of more than 100 pirate vessels and the confiscation of numerous weapons, including small arms and rocket-propelled grenades. The international coalitions operating in the Horn of Africa region have turned over approximately 1,000 pirates to law enforcement officials in various countries for prosecution. We support the Departments of State and Justice in their ongoing efforts in this area.

The Department of Defense is also working with the international "Contact Group on Piracy off the Coast of Somalia" on numerous initiatives related to industry, operational, public diplomacy, and legal issues. In terms of expanding its focus, recent discussions include exploring the possibility of pursuing the criminals who are funding pirates, demanding ransoms, and laundering the illegal proceeds from the ransom payments. Since January 2010, Somali pirates received more than $80 million in the form of ransom payments. In a country where the average annual per capita GDP is about $600, these ransoms are enormously enticing. We need to find a way to make piracy a less profitable choice. We support the Departments of State and Treasury in their ongoing efforts in this area.

Disrupting piracy will continue to be a challenge for several reasons. First, as Under Secretary of Defense for Policy Michèle Flournoy testified in 2009 to the Senate Armed Services Committee, "the root causes of Somali piracy lie in the poverty and instability that continue to plague that troubled country, and addressing these root causes will be a lengthy, complicated and difficult process." Although some areas of Somalia, specifically Somaliland and Puntland, are relatively stable, most of Somalia lacks a functioning government or established rule of law system, which contributes to the ability of pirates to plan, organize, and operate ashore with impunity. Not only can pirates operate freely from coastal fishing villages, but the dramatic increase in ransoms paid out has made piracy a lucrative business venture leading to the development of a complex network of pirates, facilitators, and financiers outside of Somalia. Over the long term, the international community's ability to combat Somali pirates in the broader Horn of Africa region will be directly linked to our ability to help Somalis increase government capacity, meet the population's basic needs, and develop law enforcement, prosecution and incarceration capabilities.

Second, the geographic area affected is vast: As I noted, Somali pirates operate in a total sea space of approximately 2.85 million square nautical miles. This is an increase of 185 percent in just the last two years. For naval or law enforcement ships and other assets, tracking a few dozen low-tech pirate skiffs and intervening to stop pirate attacks in the act that can last only a few minutes are exceptionally difficult due to the number and dispersion of pirate assets in the Arabian Sea and western Indian Ocean. Even more challenging is that these pirate vessels easily blend in with ordinary, legitimate shipping when they are not engaged in acts of piracy. In a recent trend, pirates attack dhows and use them as motherships from which to launch additional pirate attacks further out at sea and during inclement weather (particularly monsoon season). These vessels also blend in with the legitimate elements in the maritime landscape. The scale of this challenge, therefore, cannot be addressed as a military or law enforcement mission alone. Adequate coverage of the area in which Somali pirates currently operate would require more ships than are currently in the inventory of the world's navies.

Third, even when pirates are captured, often they are not successfully prosecuted and held accountable. Although piracy is a crime of "universal jurisdiction" – meaning that any State, under international law, may prosecute any piratical act – the reality is that gaps remain in the ability of many States to prosecute them. Some States still lack the appropriate domestic laws to prosecute pirates, which undermines our effort to create an effective legal deterrent. Other States have appropriate domestic legal frameworks, but lack the prosecutorial and judicial capacity to hold pirates accountable. Worse yet, other States lack the political will to take effective action.

Finally, we believe strongly that the merchant shipping fleet must be an integral partner in combating piracy. Although the merchant shipping industry has made significant improvements in on-ship security measures over the last couple years, much more must be done. Ships from all over the world transit the Gulf of Aden and use the shipping lanes along the east coast of Somalia, but some in the industry assume unrealistically that the presence of military forces obviates the need for more robust shipboard private security measures. As a result, certain members of industry have been unwilling to invest in the basic security measures that would render shipping less vulnerable to attack. Further, the insurance industry could create more financial incentives to encourage full implementation of Best Management Practices, which have proven effective in helping vessels evade or deter pirate attacks.

As part of the Department of Defense's broader counter-piracy mission set, we will continue to be prepared to respond, as appropriate, when U.S.-flagged vessels and U.S. citizens are involved or as part of our commitment to counter-piracy operations through CTF 151 and Operation OCEAN SHIELD. Our actions, however, will be most effective when private partners take proactive measures themselves. Most pirates are opportunistic criminals: whenever possible, they will focus on the easy targets and avoid the difficult targets. For example, no vessel with armed private security teams has been successfully pirated.

Again, as Under Secretary Flournoy testified, "the single most effective short-term response to piracy will be working with merchant shipping lines to ensure that vessels in

25

the region take appropriate private security measures themselves." In so vast an expanse of ocean, and with so many other critical national security priorities, it is not possible for our military to prevent or intervene in each and every pirate attack. But, with appropriate on-board security measures in place, the majority of pirate attacks can be thwarted without any need for military intervention.

Effective merchant private ship security includes an array of passive and active defensive measures. Effective passive security measures can include developing a comprehensive security plan; increasing sailing speed; conducting risk assessments; removing external ladders; posting lookouts at all times; limiting external lighting; rigging barriers (such as barbed wire and fencing) in low freeboard areas; securing hatches to limit access to crew and control spaces; creating "safe rooms"; and maintaining good communications with maritime security authorities. Rigging fire hoses to repel boarders and maintaining professional civilian armed security teams on board are active defensive measures that can mean the difference between a successful and a failed pirate attack. We note that in all cases where armed private security teams have been used, they have successfully kept pirates from boarding their vessel.

At the moment, Somali piracy appears to be motivated by money, not by ideology. Some have raised a possible connection between pirates and violent extremists groups in the region, and, although we presently do not see meaningful connections, we remain vigilant in looking for connections that may develop. Nonetheless, we know that in other contexts, narcotics production and other forms of criminal activity are sometimes "taxed" by extremist groups, as in Afghanistan. We need to ensure that piracy does not evolve into a significant funding source for violent extremist organizations.

These varied and multi-dimensional challenges should make it clear that there will be no simple solution to the growing problem of piracy in the greater Horn of Africa region. Successful cases of counter-piracy in the past have shown that the problem of piracy is not resolved exclusively by military forces operating in the maritime domain. This will ultimately hold true for any solution to the current problem in the broader Horn of Africa region. Ultimately, three major courses of action are available to counter piracy.

7

First, as I have just discussed, the shipping industry can work to make its vessels harder for pirates to target. Time and again, we have seen that implementation of best management practices or the employment of private armed security teams has contributed significantly to preventing attacks. Second, the U.S. government can work collaboratively with partner nations and the private sector to render piracy less lucrative. The financial returns from piracy are many times greater than that of most legitimate economic activity in Somalia, suggesting that piracy will not dissipate unless it becomes less profitable. The U.S. government can also address the root causes of piracy by considering how it can support the development of state capacity and good governance in Somalia – a challenge, as Undersecretary Flournoy noted, that will be lengthy and difficult.

Irrespective of how we pursue these three courses of action, the relatively low incidence of pirate hijackings when compared to total maritime traffic in the Arabian Sea and western Indian Ocean has implications for how we allocate military assets. As the members of this subcommittee know, the Department of Defense has urgent priorities around the globe, particularly in Afghanistan and Iraq. In the Horn of Africa, our existing and planned counterterrorism activities remain important to the global struggle against violent extremism. Many of the resources most in demand for counter-piracy activities, such as intelligence, surveillance, and reconnaissance assets, are the same assets that are urgently required elsewhere.

Although it is important that we find effective ways to address the growing problem of piracy—with particular attention to preventing piracy from becoming a funding source for violent extremist groups—we need to ensure that effectively addressing piracy does not come at the expense of other ongoing, critical military commitments.

The Department of Defense will continue to work with partners and regional States to develop their capacity to patrol the seas, and we will encourage them to fill gaps in their legislative frameworks so that they can prosecute pirates in their own domestic systems. Under the State Department's lead, we will also work with regional States to increase prosecutorial and judicial capacity to try pirates since effective and fair prosecutions are part of creating a long-term deterrent. And in support of our interagency partners we will work, when possible, with local authorities in Somalia to address the on-shore components of piracy, which includes tracking the on-shore facilitators and financiers and monitoring safe-havens that enable piracy on the high seas.

Many of these efforts complement our development and counterterrorism goals in the region. Although none are quick fixes, over the long term, increasing local government and law enforcement capacity and fostering sustainable economic development are all part of reducing the threat of violent extremism, as well as reducing the threat of piracy.

Mr. Chairman and members of the subcommittee, we recognize that the problem of piracy is not just a problem for Somalia. In recent years, pirate activity has also occurred in West Africa, the Strait of Malacca, and other places around the globe. Although the complete elimination of piracy on the high seas would be as difficult to achieve as the complete elimination of all robberies and assaults, we believe that we can, and must, reduce the likelihood of successful pirate attacks through deterrence, disruption, interdiction, and punishment. This will require coordinated international action and a variety of innovative public-private partnerships, but we are confident that progress can be made.

Thank you for the opportunity to testify, and I welcome your questions and comments.

Mr. ROYCE. Thank you, Mr. Wechsler.

One of the things that hasn't changed is the vastness of the ocean. The reason we established the U.S. Navy, arguably, the reason put forward by Jefferson had to do with pirate attacks off the Barbary Coast. And so what has changed over time is our rules of engagement.

And I know this is a debatable point here in the U.S. and in the U.K., but Mr. Shapiro, in a speech last year, you said, "We have to apply 21st century standards of evidence, human rights, and other legal protections" to the piracy problem. We are aware of the debates on the engagement between the way the British and the U.S. handle this and the way that the Russians, for example, and the Indians handle the piracy problem.

There has not been one pirate who has taken a Russian seaman who has lived the tell the tale. And the Indians engage the same way.

The Indian Navy, they take these ships to the bottom of the ocean.

A few weeks ago, I think it was, I read about a German warship that engaged two attack skiffs and sunk them but allowed the mother ship to return.

So the rules of engagement are different between different navies. And I think one of the questions we wrestle with, and I know reading—I have seen legal commentary put forward, that the U.N. Security Council resolutions, which were issued under Charter 7 of the U.N. Charter, should serve as sufficient legal justice to kill pirates on the high seas. And you have legal scholars calling for targeting, selective targeting of pirate leaders, just as we do with al-Qaeda, with terrorist leaders in Yemen or in Pakistan.

So, why not take this approach, Mr. Shapiro? I mean, we can revisit your commentary on this and sort of reopen this debate.

Mr. SHAPIRO. Well, thanks for that question. I think the quote you were referring to is, I was quoting Secretary Clinton saying that we needed 21st century solutions to a 19th century problem. And that meant more broadly, we need to use all the tools at our disposal.

Mr. ROYCE. Let me quote you exactly, "We have to apply 21st century standards of evidence, human rights, and other legal protections" to the piracy problem. That is sort of the debate.

Mr. SHAPIRO. I think a couple of issues, first, from our perspective, our ability to gain international support for addressing piracy will require us to treat in a manner consistent with the rule of law.

Secondly, when you talk about targeting pirates on the high seas, it is important to prosecute those we catch. But what is more important is to target the pirate facilitators because there is an almost innumerable number of young pirates who are willing to be recruited to go out on the high seas and take their chances, given their life in Somalia.

It is the facilitators and the people who profit from this that we need to target, and that is what our approach is going to start to do.

We have already brought back two facilitators back to the United States for prosecution. And I think that in order to continue to get the level of international support that we need to make further progress, that is the right approach.

We continue to build cases against them, as we have done against other organized crime groups, such as drug cartels, build the cases, bring them back for prosecution, and in that way, we can disrupt the pirates from being able to get the funding that they need to go out to sea.

Mr. ROYCE. You know, it is an interesting question. I remember the debate in the State Senate over the use of lethal force, which is what we are talking about here, as well, in California. The question was—and it actually prevailed at the time—the question was, could you use lethal force if someone was attacking you, coming into your home, robbing your home, invading your home, could you use lethal force? And the decision in the State Senate and the Assembly was, yes, you could.

And clearly, the conclusion that has been reached in Germany, India, Russia, is that they are going to use lethal force in engagements with pirates.

Mr. SHAPIRO. Well, in India, they did use lethal force to free their ship, but they also brought back many of their pirates for prosecution in India.

And I would say, Secretary Clinton has expressed a desire to make progress. She has expressed an openness to entertaining ideas regarding addressing the pirate problem on shore.

But at the end of the day, if we are to target these networks, it will be important to build cases and develop information, and that means you bring in one pirate facilitator, and then he rolls up the next one. And then you bring in the next one and work your way up the chain to the highest levels. So these require long, complicated cases. But at the end of the day, if we are going to disrupt these networks, we are going to have to target the appropriate people, bring them back, get them to turn on their higher ups and continue to make progress in disrupting these organizations.

Mr. ROYCE. Mr. Sherman. Thank you.

Mr. SHERMAN. Mr. Shapiro, the State Department has to often decide, do they want to be popular with the diplomats from Europe, or do they want to serve the interests of the American people?

These ships, 99.9 percent of them, are foreign ships. They are not U.S. ships. They are not U.S. crews. We don't get the jobs, and most of that cargo isn't headed to the United States.

And yet these are foreign shipowners, making foreign profits.

Do we charge any fees for protection for any of these ships? Or do we bear the cost at the cost of the U.S. taxpayer?

Mr. SHAPIRO. We do not charge fees.

Mr. SHERMAN. And so we will use the marginal cost system to say that this is only costing us hundreds of millions, but it is actually costing us billions, a gift to foreign shipowners.

You say that punishing the rank and file pirates doesn't matter; I think, yes, there are a large number of Somalis who are willing to become rank and file pirates, but that is because they don't get punished. If you create a high level of mortality among these rank and file pirates, that will be successful.

But now let's turn to the real rip off of the U.S. taxpayer, and that is these shipowners. They don't want to told to put armed guards. That costs them money. They would rather have U.S. tax-payers pay money. They don't want to be told, only go through in convoys. That costs them money. They want our money.

What are you doing to say, we are going to shift the costs to the shipowners, we are going to require armed guards, and we are going to require armed convoys?

Mr. SHAPIRO. Well I would say for U.S. ships, you know, the Coast Guard——

Mr. SHERMAN. None of these are U.S. ships, sir, so why don't you talk about the real ships?

Mr. SHAPIRO. Well, obviously, we are working through the Contact Group and through our international partners to encourage this.

We, as a matter of policy, have made the decision that for U.S. ships, we will permit it. A number of other states actually ban it. Some ships have moved their flag states because their governments will not allow them. And we are working through diplomatic channels to change that attitude.

Mr. SHERMAN. So as long as it is in the interests of the shipowners and the Europeans, so that the shipowners don't have to bear the cost of having armed guards and the shipowners don't have to bear the cost of going in convoys, we will be there with U.S. taxpayer money to support these shipowners?

Mr. SHAPIRO. Well, I think we are there with U.S. taxpayer money because it is in our own interests. As we saw——

Mr. SHERMAN. It is in our interests to bear the costs that should be borne by those foreign shipowners?

Mr. SHAPIRO. Well, it is in our interests as we saw, you know, we had four Americans who were brutally murdered by pirates. We have U.S. ships that have had been attacked by pirates. So it is—there is——

Mr. SHERMAN. And if these ships were all required to go in convoys, those Americans would be alive, and the costs for corporate shipowners would be higher. Is that correct?

Mr. SHAPIRO. In terms of—probably that, I believe that is an accurate statement. But I am not an expert on what the shipowners think their costs are.

But I would say, certainly we have been disappointed. And Secretary Clinton has testified that she has been disappointed that the shipowners have not taken more responsibility, and that is going to be a focus of our efforts going forward is to put——

Mr. SHERMAN. I serve on Financial Services, where we get a chance to bail out rich corporations with U.S. taxpayer dollars. We rarely get the opportunity to discuss that in this room. But these are multi-billion dollar private corporations who don't want to bear the costs. They don't want to bear the inconvenience. They don't want to pay for armed guards. They don't want the inefficiency of having to go in convoys, and they are willing to operate that way because they are subsidized by free security offered by the U.S. taxpayer.

I would say it is time for us to condition our protection of these ships on them either paying the fee or bearing the cost. And if U.S. ships are in the area, we could organize convoys. But bailouts happen, apparently, in the jurisdiction of both of my committees.

Mr. SHAPIRO. I would make two points.

First, we have seen more and more shipowners adopt the practice of armed security teams. Indeed, that is why we think there has been less success over the last 3 months, is that greater adherence to best management practices.

The problem is that the small number of ships that don't follow best management practices are responsible for the vast majority of those that are actually pirated. So the question is, what do you do about those? And we need to work with the shipping industry to put financial pressure and incentives on those who are not following best management practices and leading to this problem to take further action.

Mr. SHERMAN. I would point out that the U.S. Navy is capable of detaining those ships that are acting in a way that is hazardous to their crews, promoting piracy, putting themselves in a position where they are going to need a naval bailout. And for these ships not to be willing to have armed guards and/or convoys and for us to sit back and say, okay, we will defend you, is bailout foreign policy.

I yield back.

Mr. ROYCE. Mr. Duncan, I have an amendment on the floor. If you will continue to chair and handle the panel here, I will try to return after it is taken up.

I think you are next, Mr. Duncan.

Mr. DUNCAN [presiding]. Thank you.

I recognize myself for 5 minutes.

I believe that the presence of U.S. Naval vessels in the region are a definite deterrent and meeting with Admiral Papp with the Coast Guard recently and learning that the U.S. does have a strong presence there with the Coast Guard is encouraging.

But I think it was French philosopher Pascal that said a police force without force is impotent.

And I believe that if we don't have a presence there—I think you mentioned earlier that the Germans and the Russians and the Indians even use more force in dealing with the Somali pirates, and I would be willing to say their vessels are probably the least pirated. So I would love to see that.

I want you to, if you will repeat, did you say that you would encourage security forces on U.S. flag vessels?

Mr. SHAPIRO. Well, the Coast Guard requires either an armed or unarmed security team for U.S. flag vessels. We have not taken a position on whether to encourage them to be armed or unarmed other than to note that armed vessels have not been successfully pirated.

Mr. DUNCAN. Okay. And that is good.

Mr. Wechsler, you noted that you didn't see a meaningful connection between the pirates and other violent extremist groups, and we are all concerned about money going to the extremists and the jihadists that are wanting to continue to wage this war against freedom.

But there been meaningful reports that multi-million dollar ransoms have become a source of funding for Somali based terrorist groups al-Shabaab, and they have reportedly taxed Somali pirate ransoms. The Kenyan Government estimates that 30 percent of ransom payments are funneled to al-Shabaab.

Could you comment on that? And does the Kenyan Government have it wrong?

Mr. WECHSLER. Sure. Let me make sure that I am clear.

I want to make two points about what I can say in this session, and if you want to get together in a closed session, one on one, I am happy to give a full intelligence brief on this as well.

What we don't believe, what we don't see yet is operational or organizational alignment between the piracy, the pirates themselves and al-Shabaab. They are not the same organization.

Mr. DUNCAN. No direct connection then?

Mr. WECHSLER. It is not no direct connection, but they are not the same organization; they are not operationally or organizationally aligned.

What we do believe that we see some evidence of is coercion. So these are competing organizations, and al-Shabaab sometimes coerces the pirates into giving some revenues to them. That is, again, with all the caveats that I said previously about the limits of our intelligence right now, that is what I can say in this open session.

Mr. DUNCAN. Thank you.

The chair will recognize the gentleman from New York 5 minutes.

Mr. HIGGINS. Thank you, Mr. Chairman.

United States Special Forces killed three Somali pirates in 2009 and freed captain Richard Phillips. In that there are dozens of ships being held off the coast of Somalia and some 300 to 500 merchant sailors, why aren't other countries taking unilateral action against these pirates in the Gulf of Aden?

Mr. SHAPIRO. Well, each country makes its own decisions about how they will address their pirated vessels.

We have, as was noted earlier, certain countries have become more aggressive in addressing their pirated vessels where their citizens have been captured and their ships have been captured. India was mentioned; South Korea, and others.

Ultimately, because often these vessels have hostages, each case is unique. Each case has its own particular factors which require the Navy ship on scene to make a determination as to whether it is, the risk is worth taking kinetic action against those ships. So there is no hard and fast rule. Each is unique, based on each particular circumstance.

Mr. WECHSLER. I think I can best describe what we do, and I also want to make sure that this point is clear for this committee, because it is quite an important point about our rules of engagement. We are constantly assessing and reassessing our rules of engagement. Again, the specific nature of our rules of engagement is something that I would be more than happy to discuss in a closed or one-on-one session with anyone here.

But I am very comfortable with the rules of engagement as they are now. They are very well balanced. We are constantly assessing them. They have been changed as a result of the changing dynamic. That I can say in this session.

And one thing I would just point out is, as recently as last month, May 16th, the USS Bulkeley responded to a mayday message from the Artemis Glory, which reported that it was being attacked by pirates, launched an SH–60B helicopter. Upon its arrival, under the principle of extended unit self defense, which is allowed in order to provide protection to the crew, the helicopter engaged the pirates. All the pirates are believed to have been killed.

So I do want to make clear that some of the distinctions that folks may be referring to between what we do and what some other countries do, we have very robust rules of engagement, and when appropriate, we can act, and we do act.

But I do want to go back, again, to what I said in my opening statement; the full solution to this problem will not be addressed by military means alone. It will be addressed by some of the other nonmilitary elements that we have also been discussing here.

Mr. HIGGINS. Just a final question. Are there concerns along the Gulf of Aden and the Horn of Africa that this problem is expanding to areas beyond Somalia?

Mr. SHAPIRO. Thus far, we have not seen it. Obviously, the ships coming from Somalia are moving further and further out into the Indian Ocean. But in terms of pirate havens, typically that takes place, as we have seen in Somalia, in a failed state environment. So we have not seen this tactic spreading elsewhere in the region. However, we are concerned that the number of—that the ships are extending their range to cover a broader area of the Indian Ocean.

Mr. HIGGINS. Okay.

Mr. WECHSLER. Somalia is a special case. In some parts of the world, it is—and going through history, some of which has been mentioned before, piracy, including back in the early 1800s, was, in effect, a state-sponsored activity. There was somebody making a decision to do this. And in fact, at that point, a huge proportion of the U.S. Treasury was going to pay tribute to the pirates in Tripoli because it was a state-sponsored activity.

In other places, where there was a—where it is nonstate activities, it is much more geographically focused, as it has been in the Straits of Malacca. Here you have the combination of a vast geographic area and no state, in large case, to organize this, and so a sanctuary for the pirates. So this is the combination of both of these situations for the worst-case scenario.

Mr. DUNCAN. The chair now recognizes the gentlewoman from North Carolina, Ms. Ellmers, for 5 minutes.

Mrs. ELLMERS. Thank you. Thank you gentlemen for being here today.

Mr. Shapiro, I have a question. We have talked a lot about the Somalian pirates, and U.S. officials, yourselves, acknowledge the fact that we need to be doing more to alleviate this problem.

One of the areas, of course, is targeting and following the monetary flow of ransom and the moneys that are being paid. In a recent meeting of the International Contact Group, they did discuss mapping and following the money. But the group was put together in 2009. This seems like a pretty commonsense approach.

Why is it taking this long to prioritize that and to take this approach?

Mr. SHAPIRO. I will say, as you mentioned, the Contact Group was set up in 2009. And initially, it was starting from scratch, and it was focusing on building prosecutorial capacity, working on what and how to work, how the international community should coordinate on this issue.

As we learned more, as we learned how the pirates operate, it has become apparent that in order to be successful, we will need to target the financial flows.

There has been a learning curve for the international community, no question about it.

But now we have ascended that learning curve. And we in the United States Government, at the State Department, we have begun to devote resources into how to crack this. We are going to work with our interagency partners, and the Contact Group is talking about setting up a fifth working group on financial flows, so that we can work together with the international community which will be essential.

Mrs. ELLMERS. Mr. Wechsler, kind of along the same line of questioning here. Basically, you have pointed out that the Department of Defense is working with the International Contact Group with the aim of pursuing criminals who are funding pirates, demanding ransoms, and laundering the illegal proceeds from ransom payments. In your opinion, how can this best be executed?

Mr. WECHSLER. The Department of Defense has learned a lot, has been forced to learn a lot about this question in Iraq and Afghanistan where, we have confronted and are confronting an irregular adversary with independent sources of revenue through criminal means. The best way to go about this and the way that I know my colleague from the Department of State would agree is to use all the tools available to government in a coordinated campaign effort to go against the financiers on a counter network capacity.

You have to be able to map the networks. You have to be able to identify the right nodes, and then you have to be able to identify which tool of the U.S. Government is best suited to go after the nodes to have—what kind of effect that you want to have, whether it is military activity, whether it is intelligence activity, it is law enforcement activity, whether it is sanctioning activity. That is the way that we have found in other contexts the ability to have some strategic impact.

Mrs. ELLMERS. Thank you.

And I yield back my time.

Mr. DUNCAN. Thank you.

I am going to reserve some time for myself to ask another question for Chairman Royce. The Somali piracy is essentially an international criminal enterprise, and the GAO found that the information on private finances collected by various U.S. Government agencies is not being systematically analyzed and is unclear if any agency is using it to identify and apprehend pirate leaders or financiers. How are you correcting this?

Because we have had practice with organized crime and terrorism, this is where we can truly have a strategic impact it would seem. So the question is, how are you correcting this? And that is for either one.

Mr. SHAPIRO. As I mentioned, the State Department is coordinating interagency efforts to identify the most effective means of disrupting the financial flows of piracy and targeting the pirate——

Mr. DUNCAN. Would that be the Contact Group?

Mr. SHAPIRO. Yes. We will work both in our Government, as well as with international partners. And through our international partners is with the Contact Group. So we will be working—you know, there are a number of agencies throughout the U.S. Government, the Department of Treasury, Defense, DEA, FBI, as well as the intelligence community. We will also be working with INTERPOL and through our law enforcement contacts.

So we do acknowledge that we need to do a better job on this—no question about it—that we need to focus on financial flows and that we need to devote the resources that are necessary in the U.S. Government to better track financial flows.

Mr. DUNCAN. When you say we will be working, I understand that the Contact Group was established over 2 years ago and with the things going on in the world, it would seem like this element would be prioritized.

Mr. SHAPIRO. And indeed, there was a recent meeting, as the Congresswoman mentioned, to talk about this issue at the Contact Group. And the goal was to set up another working group to focus on financial flows. So there is great interest in the international community. And I have talked with a number of our international partners who are greatly interested in working with us on tracking financial flows.

Mr. DUNCAN. As you can see, I am the last one here. So let me take this opportunity to thank the panelists for being here. If any of our subcommittee members or committee members have written questions, they will be submitted, and we ask you to timely return those. And since there is no other committee members here, we will stand adjourned. Thank you.

[Whereupon, at 3:04 p.m., the subcommittee was adjourned.]

APPENDIX

SUBCOMMITTEE HEARING NOTICE
COMMITTEE ON FOREIGN AFFAIRS
U.S. HOUSE OF REPRESENTATIVES
WASHINGTON, D.C.

Subcommittee on Terrorism, Nonproliferation, and Trade
Edward R. Royce (R-CA), Chairman

June 14, 2011

You are respectfully requested to attend an OPEN hearing of the Subcommittee on Terrorism, Nonproliferation, and Trade, to be held in **Room 2172 of the Rayburn House Office Building (and available live, via the WEBCAST link on the Committee website at http://www.hcfa.house.gov):**

DATE: Wednesday, June 15, 2011

TIME: 2:00 p.m.

SUBJECT: Global Maritime Piracy: Fueling Terrorism, Harming Trade

WITNESSES: **Panel I**

Mr. Andrew J. Shapiro
Assistant Secretary
Bureau of Political-Military Affairs
U.S. Department of State

Mr. William F. Wechsler
Deputy Assistant Secretary
Counternarcotics and Global Threats
U.S. Department of Defense

By Direction of the Chairman

The Committee on Foreign Affairs seeks to make its facilities accessible to persons with disabilities. If you are in need of special accommodations, please call 202/225-5021 at least four business days in advance of the event, whenever practicable. Questions with regard to special accommodations in general (including availability of Committee materials in alternative formats and assistive listening devices) may be directed to the Committee.

———————

COMMITTEE ON FOREIGN AFFAIRS

MINUTES OF SUBCOMMITTEE ON _____ *Terrorism, Nonproliferation, and Trade* _____ HEARING

Day __*Wednesday*__ Date __*June 15, 2011*__ Room _____ *2172* _____

Starting Time ___ *2:06 pm* ___ Ending Time ___ *3:15 pm* _

Recesses ____ (____ to ____)(____ to ____)(____ to ____)(____ to ____)(____ to ____)(____to ____)

Presiding Member(s)

Rep. Ed Royce, Chairman

Check all of the following that apply:

Open Session ☑
Executive (closed) Session ☐
Televised ☑

Electronically Recorded (taped) ☑
Stenographic Record ☑

TITLE OF HEARING:

"Global Maritime Piracy: Fueling Terrorism, Harming Trade"

SUBCOMMITTEE MEMBERS PRESENT:

Reps. Royce, Sherman, Poe, Higgins, Duncan, Connolly, Ellmers

NON-SUBCOMMITTEE MEMBERS PRESENT: *(Mark with an * if they are not members of full committee.)*

HEARING WITNESSES: Same as meeting notice attached? Yes ☑ No ☐
(If "no", please list below and include title, agency, department, or organization.)

STATEMENTS FOR THE RECORD: *(List any statements submitted for the record.)*

Rep. Connolly

TIME SCHEDULED TO RECONVENE _____
or
TIME ADJOURNED _____

Subcommittee Staff Director

Terrorism, Nonproliferation, and Trade Subcommittee
Member Attendance

Republicans

☑ Rep. Edward Royce (Chair)

☑ Rep. Ted Poe

☑ Rep. Jeff Duncan

☐ Rep. Bill Johnson

☐ Rep. Tim Griffin

☐ Rep. Ann Marie Buerkle

☑ Rep. Renee Ellmers

Democrats

☑ Rep. Brad Sherman (Ranking Member)

☐ Rep. David Cicilline

☑ Rep. Gerry Connolly

☑ Rep. Brian Higgins

☐ Rep. Allyson Schwartz

41

The Honorable Gerald E. Connolly (VA-11)

TNT Subcommittee Hearing
Global Maritime Piracy: Fueling Terrorism, Harming Trade
Wednesday June 15, 2011
2pm

In recent years, a perfect storm of events have fostered an environment where maritime piracy is rampant. The crime—which costs the global economy anywhere from $7 billion to $12 billion—is concentrated off the Horn of Africa, where over 33,000 commercial ships traverse the Gulf of Aden each year. The lack of rule of law and governance in Somalia—particularly the northern semi-autonomous region of Puntland—has provided a base of operations for Somali pirate networks. Authorities in Puntland have directly colluded with pirates; a 2010 U.N. Monitoring Group report stated that key leaders in the Puntland administration have received money from piracy and in some cases have extended protection to pirate militias.

According to several reports accompanying United Nations Security Council resolutions, there are several distinct "pirate action groups" concentrated on the northern coast of Puntland. These groups have launched attacks from the same areas in which Al Shabaab operates. The pirate groups operate in small teams equipped with AK-47s and rocket propelled grenade (RPG) launchers. They often have a larger mother ship equipped with additional supplies, along with one or more smaller boats that approach the targeted ship.

Perhaps in order to soften their image, some pirate groups claim they are more of a civilian coast guard—a dubious description, given the financial payoff of piracy. One ship can yield a ransom of millions of dollars. Just last fall, pirates received the highest payout to date—$9.5 million for the release of a South Korean oil tanker. Other ships have yielded a king's ransom as well—$3 million for a Saudi oil supertanker in 2009, $4 million for a Chinese coal carrier, and $7 million for a Greek supertanker. The list goes on.

While piracy has been a crime of violence, recent instances are particularly troubling. In February, four Americans were shot and killed aboard their sailboat, the *Quest*, after Somali pirates hijacked the boat off the coast of Oman. Details remain sketchy, though initial U.S. Navy reports indicated that the pirates fired an RPG at one of the Navy destroyers that was participating in hostage negotiations. The fourteen surviving pirates were indicted by a jury in Norfolk, Virginia.

To add insult to injury, these pirates' brazenness is only exceeded by their extreme sense of entitlement. In April of 2009, Somali pirates hijacked the *Maersk Alabama*, a U.S.-flagged ship contracted to deliver USAID food assistance to Somalia. After U.S. Special Forces killed three of the pirates and mounted a rescue operation, a leader of the pirate group told reporters that American citizens would be hunted down in retaliation for what happened on the *Maersk*. That same month, pirates attacked another U.S.-flagged aid ship—the *Liberty Sun*—purely for retaliation for what happened on the *Maersk*. The fact that the pirates were the aggressors apparently was irrelevant. Moreover, pirates have unsuccessfully attempted to attack the *Maersk* again on two separate occasions.

When pirates are targeting U.S.-flagged ships purely in retaliation for American self defense, the problem has truly come to a head. I look forward to today's testimony regarding U.S. actions in combating this scourge on the high seas.

SUBCOMMITTEE ON TERRORISM, NONPROLIFERATION, AND TRADE

Edward R. Royce (R-CA), Chairman

Wednesday, June 15, 2011

Global Maritime Piracy: Fueling Terrorism, Harming Trade

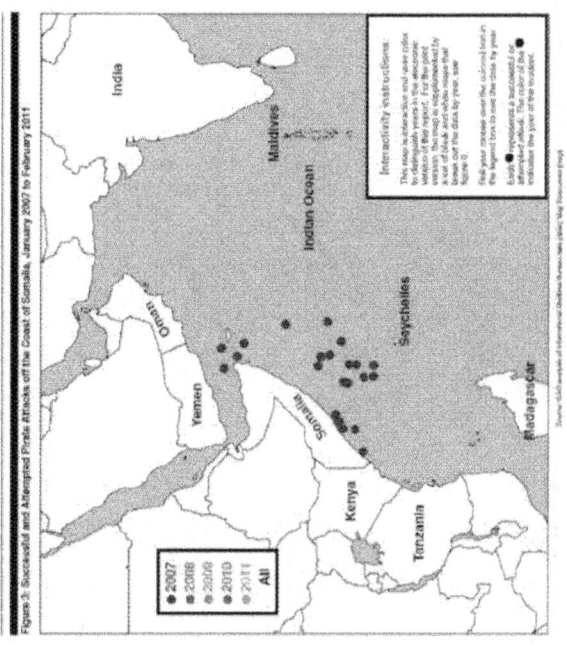

2007

Figure 3: Successful and Attempted Pirate Attacks off the Coast of Somalia, January 2007 to February 2011

44

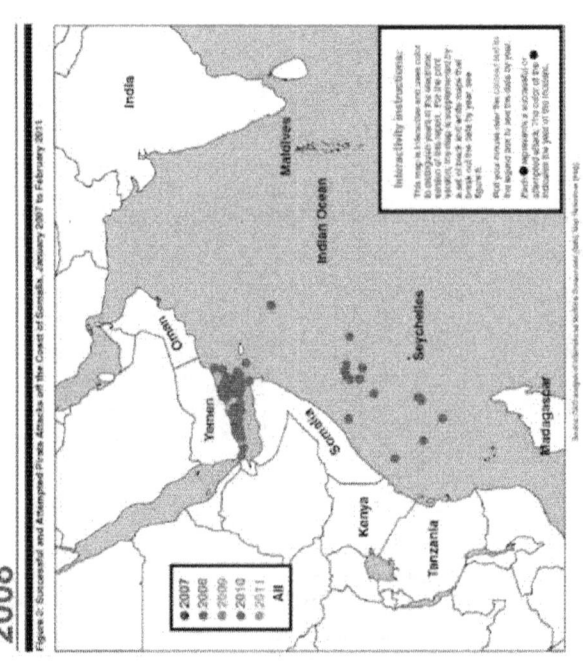

Figure 2: Successful and Attempted Pirate Attacks off the Coast of Somalia, January 2007 to February 2011

45

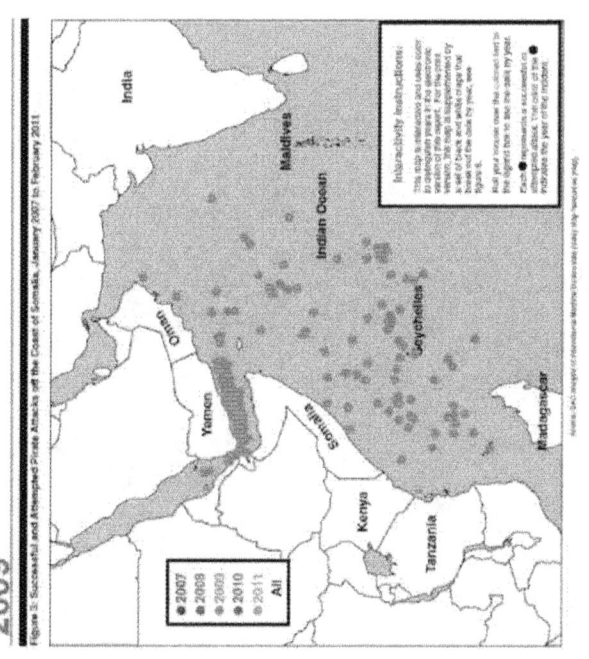

2009

Figure 3: Successful and Attempted Pirate Attacks off the Coast of Somalia, January 2007 to February 2011

46

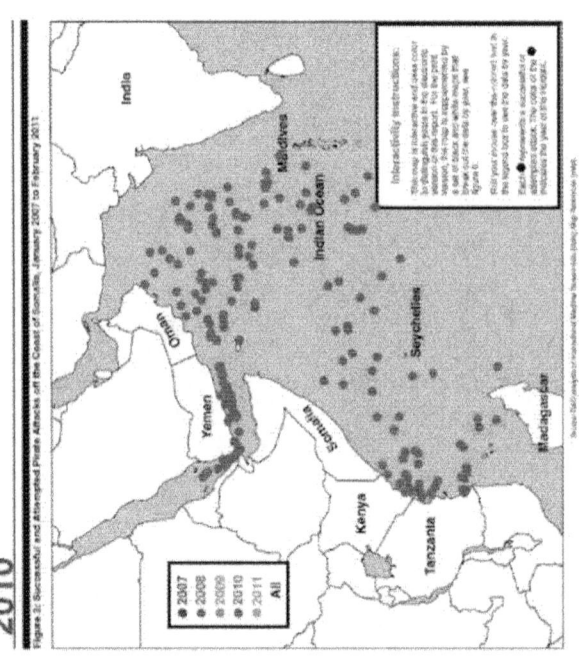

2010

Figure 3: Successful and Attempted Pirate Attacks off the Coast of Somalia, January 2007 to February 2011

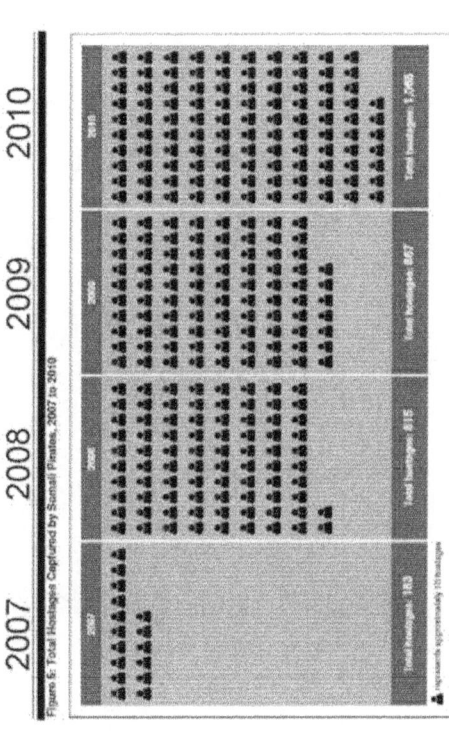

Figure 6: Total Hostages Captured by Somali Pirates, 2007 to 2010

Total Hostages Captured by Somali Pirates, 2007 to 2010

48

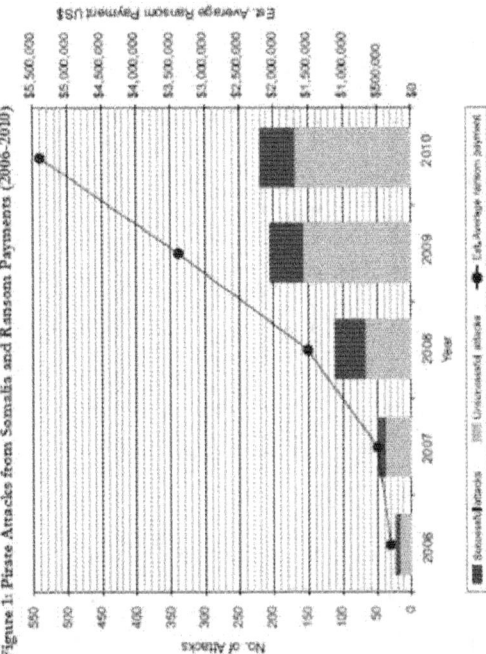

Figure 1: Pirate Attacks from Somalia and Ransom Payments (2006-2010)

Rise of Ransom Payments (2006-2010)